WORLD WAR I

AIRCRAFT
OF WORLD WAR I

BY
JOHN HAMILTON

Abdo & Daughters
An imprint of Abdo Publishing | abdopublishing.com

abdopublishing.com

Published by Abdo Publishing, a division of ABDO, PO Box 398166, Minneapolis, Minnesota 55439. Copyright © 2018 by Abdo Consulting Group, Inc. International copyrights reserved in all countries. No part of this book may be reproduced in any form without written permission from the publisher. Abdo & Daughters™ is a trademark and logo of Abdo Publishing.

Printed in the United States of America, North Mankato, Minnesota.
112017
012018

THIS BOOK CONTAINS
RECYCLED MATERIALS

Editor: Sue Hamilton
Graphic Design: Sue Hamilton
Cover Design: Candice Keimig and Pakou Moua
Cover Photo: Getty
Interior Images: Alamy-pgs 13, 15, 20-21, 30-31 & 36; Getty-pgs 4, 5, 34, 38 & 40; G.H. Davis (artist)-pg 11; Granger-pgs 22-23; iStock-pg 1; Mark Miller-pgs 16-17; National Archives-pgs 12 & 26 (inset); National Museum of the U.S. Air Force-pg 39 (top); Paul Lengelle (artist)-pg 33; Rosebud's WWI Aviation Image Archive-pg 19; Shutterstock-pg 3; Smithsonian Institute-pgs 8-9 & 39 (inset); The Image Works-pgs 6-7, 14, 24-25, 26-27, 35 & 42; Wikimedia-pgs 18, 19 & 28.

Publisher's Cataloging-in-Publication Data

Names: Hamilton, John, author.
Title: Aircraft of World War I / by John Hamilton.
Description: Minneapolis, Minnesota : Abdo Publishing, 2018. | Series: World War I | Includes online resources and index.
Identifiers: LCCN 2017946719 | ISBN 9781532112850 (lib.bdg.) | ISBN 9781532150715 (ebook)
Subjects: LCSH: World War, 1914-1918--Aerial operations--Juvenile literature. | World War, 1914-1918--Equipment and supplies--Juvenile literature. | Airplanes, Military--Juvenile literature. | World War, 1914-1918--United States--Juvenile literature.
Classification: DDC 940.44--dc23
LC record available at https://lccn.loc.gov/2017946719

CONTENTS

KNIGHTS OF THE SKY

World War I introduced a new invention to the battlefield—the airplane. Slow and fragile at first, airplanes evolved in just a few short years into swift and deadly weapons of war. They were used to bomb and spy on the enemy. Ace pilots also engaged in aerial dogfights to take control of the skies.

The soldiers of World War I fought a new kind of war. Instead of facing the enemy, millions were forced to take shelter in muddy trenches. Artillery shells rained down, launched by an unseen foe. Machine guns and hidden snipers killed anyone daring or foolish enough to set foot in no-man's-land. Neither side was used to fighting this way. Honor and heroism didn't seem to have a place in this modern kind of warfare.

Every day, however, soldiers could look up and see airplanes dueling overhead. These new machines buzzed through the sky with lightning speed.

Troops on the ground cheer as an airplane zooms overhead. World War I pilots spotted enemy locations and told artillery operators where to fire their guns. Airplanes were also used to drop bombs and fire machine guns at targets on the ground.

Allied flyboys battle a squadron of German planes.

High above the battlefields of World War I, dashing pilots swooped and soared in their flying machines. The roar of engines and the staccato rattle of machine guns filled the air as wood-and-canvas airplanes performed a deadly dance in the sky. Here was fighting that soldiers stuck in muddy trenches could understand: men battling and outwitting each other, often so close they could see the faces of their enemies. World War I pilots were called "knights of the sky." They seemed to come from a time long ago, when warriors in shining armor lived their lives with chivalry and courage.

The best pilots were called aces. They fought in the freedom of the clear blue sky, where heroes were born and brave men could die with honor. The aces of World War I became legends: Mick Mannock from Great Britain, Eddie Rickenbacker from the United States, France's René Fonck, Canada's Billy Bishop, and the most famous ace of the war, Germany's Manfred von Richthofen, also known as the Red Baron.

In reality, the career of most World War I pilots was short and brutal. Their training was usually limited. Their airplanes were often unreliable, or outmatched by the enemy. Within a few short weeks of arriving at the front lines, most young pilots were shot down or died in an accident. Death at the hands of the enemy could be especially cruel. Parachutes were rare. When a plane went down in flames, the pilot faced a terrible choice: burn to death, or jump and plummet to the ground. The life of a pilot, many discovered, was not so glamorous after all. Airplanes, pilots joked, were merely coffins with wings.

EARLY AIRCRAFT

"We do not consider that aeroplanes will be of any possible use for war purposes." –Richard Haldane, British Secretary of State for War, 1910

When fighting broke out in World War I, powered aircraft had been flying for barely a decade. On December 17, 1903, Orville and Wilbur Wright flew their first plane, *Flyer 1*, at Kitty Hawk, North Carolina. The flight lasted 12 seconds, for a distance of 120 feet (37 m).

Within five years, the brothers developed a military version of their airplane. It could stay aloft for more than an hour and reach a speed of more than 40 miles per hour (64 kph). However, the United States Army couldn't decide the best way to use flying machines on the battlefield.

Meanwhile, aircraft development continued, especially in France, Great Britain, and Germany. But even in these countries, military people didn't understand how important airplanes would become. Marshall Ferdinand Foch, commander in chief of the Allied forces during World War I, once said, "The aircraft is all very well for sport, but for the army it is useless."

The 1909 Wright Military Flyer was the world's first military airplane. It was designed with two seats: one for the pilot and one for an observer.

Bleriot XI

By the time World War I started in 1914, airplane design was still in its infancy. Flying machines were slow, underpowered, and unarmed. The French Bleriot XI was a fragile plane with a weak engine that often broke down. But even with these weaknesses, in 1909 it became the first plane to cross the English Channel. The Bleriot was also the first plane to go to war, when Italian forces fought Turkey in 1911. French and British forces used planes of this type in 1914 and 1915, until aircraft with more powerful engines were developed.

The airplanes of World War I were simple machines with frames built of wood or aluminum. The frames were wrapped in canvas or linen covered in varnish, which easily caught fire. The first planes were "pusher"-type aircraft. They had the engine and propeller in back, which "pushed" the aircraft forward. Later planes had the engine and propeller mounted in front. These "pulled" the aircraft forward. This system was found to be more efficient, caused less vibration, and less noise.

The simplicity of early aircraft sometimes made them difficult to shoot down. Bullets often passed harmlessly through the thin fabric skin. Still, flying a World War I airplane was extremely hazardous. If bullets struck a gas tank, the plane might burst into flames. Another common hazard occurred when a plane went into a steep, high-speed dive. As the wind rushed past, the wings were often ripped off.

As airplanes improved, they became sturdier and more dependable. But it was still extremely dangerous being a World War I pilot, especially those with little training. In 1915, the average life expectancy of an Allied pilot on the Western Front was only 11 days.

A German plane is hit and begins a steep dive to the ground.

SCOUTS

When World War I began, airplanes were mainly used to find the location of enemy soldiers. This important job is called *reconnaissance*. With planes overhead spotting the enemy, large guns called artillery could be directed to fire more accurately. Planes could also detect large groups of enemy troops as they moved into position to launch attacks.

In the past, cavalry was used for reconnaissance. But during World War I, men on horses were easy targets for long-range snipers or machine guns. Also, horses along the Western Front could not easily travel through the maze of muddy trenches and barbed wire. Airplanes had freedom of movement. They quickly became an important replacement for horses. When the weather was good, pilots could easily spot the enemy and take photographs for the war planners on the ground to study.

When the war began in August 1914, Germany had the largest air service, even though it included only 232 aircraft. Great Britain had 113 aircraft, and France had 138. As the war progressed, each country produced airplanes by the thousands. France alone made almost 68,000 aircraft. Of those planes, nearly 53,000 were shot down or crashed.

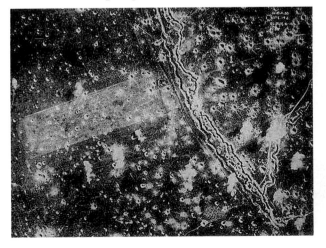

A crater-filled battlefield photographed from an Allied reconnaissance plane.

A camera is loaded on a British plane to record enemy movements and defenses.

A French scouting plane takes shots at an enemy German plane.

The first planes used in World War I were called "scouts." That name was used even during the later years of the war, when airplanes also served as fighters and bombers. In addition to their reconnaissance duties, scouts sometimes dropped small hand-held bombs on enemy troops or buildings, but they weren't very accurate. They also sometimes dropped hundreds of steel darts, called flechettes, onto troops on the ground or in trenches.

Sometimes scouts flew close to enemy planes. When they passed each other in the air, opposing pilots often smiled and waved to each other. However, this friendliness didn't last for long. Pilots soon realized that the information the enemy was gathering was hurting their fellow soldiers. Whoever controlled the skies had a big advantage on the battlefield.

Aircrews began throwing heavy objects, like bricks, at enemy planes. They also shot at them with shotguns, rifles, or pistols. Machine guns soon appeared on two-seater planes. Passengers, whose main job was to spot the enemy ground troops, could also shoot at planes.

Troops on the ground fired at enemy airplanes, but the aircraft were usually too fast or too high. Soon, antiaircraft guns were developed. They fired shells that exploded in midair. Jagged pieces of metal, called shrapnel, flew in all directions. The shrapnel was often called Archie. At times it could be deadly, but it wasn't very accurate during World War I. Soldiers on the ground complained that shrapnel falling back to Earth was more dangerous to them than to the airplanes being fired at.

Sometimes, Archie hit its target, with lethal results. British flyer Arthur Gould Lee was fighting German planes during the Battle of Cambrai in November 1917 when his plane's engine was hit by shrapnel. He glided safely to the ground. He then watched as more planes were hit by antiaircraft fire. He later wrote, "I saw something I'd never seen before… A machine was hit by a shell and blown to fragments. Bits of it fell quickly, like the engine and pilot's body, but most of it seemed to float down lazily like leaves from trees in autumn."

An American antiaircraft gun crew scans the skies for enemy planes.

ANATOMY OF AN ALBATROS D.VA

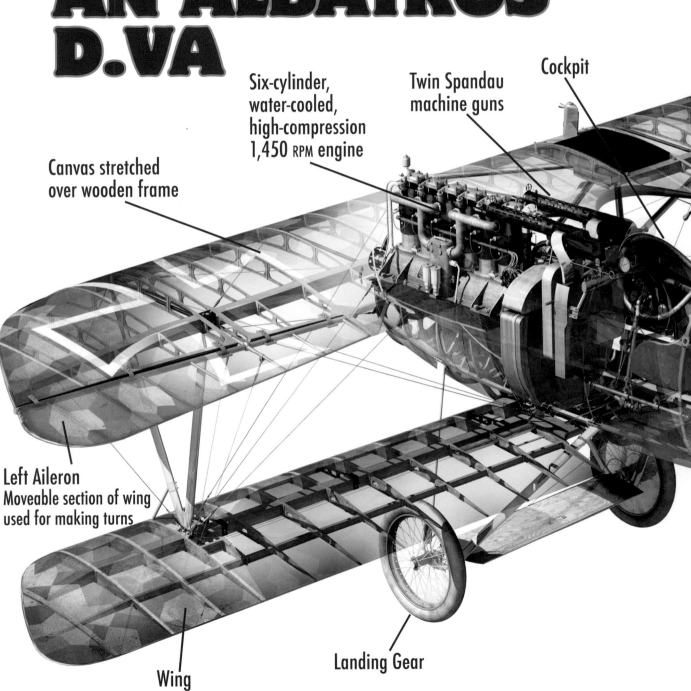

Six-cylinder, water-cooled, high-compression 1,450 RPM engine

Twin Spandau machine guns

Cockpit

Canvas stretched over wooden frame

Left Aileron
Moveable section of wing used for making turns

Wing

Landing Gear

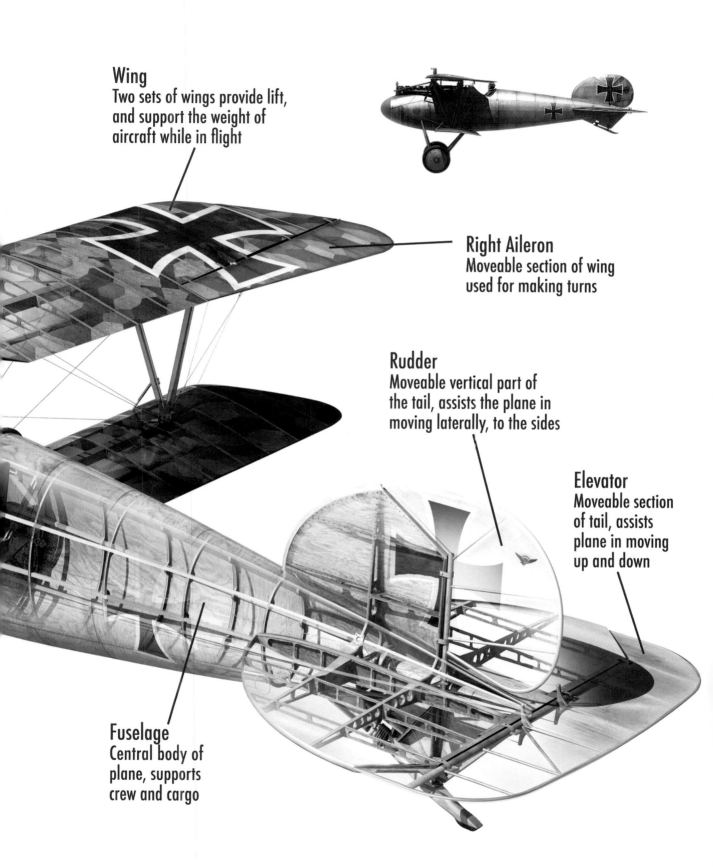

Wing
Two sets of wings provide lift, and support the weight of aircraft while in flight

Right Aileron
Moveable section of wing used for making turns

Rudder
Moveable vertical part of the tail, assists the plane in moving laterally, to the sides

Elevator
Moveable section of tail, assists plane in moving up and down

Fuselage
Central body of plane, supports crew and cargo

THE FOKKER SCOURGE

Even though antiaircraft guns were sometimes effective against scouts, both sides quickly realized they needed special planes to shoot down the enemy. These aircraft were called fighters. They were sturdy and fitted with powerful engines.

Fighters became much more effective when machine guns were mounted on the front of the planes. Now pilots could simply steer their aircraft in the direction they wanted to aim. This made it much easier to strike enemy aircraft.

One big problem remained: finding a way to shoot bullets through the arc of the whirling propeller blades. Most bullets passed safely through, but enough hit the wooden blade that sometimes it would splinter and break.

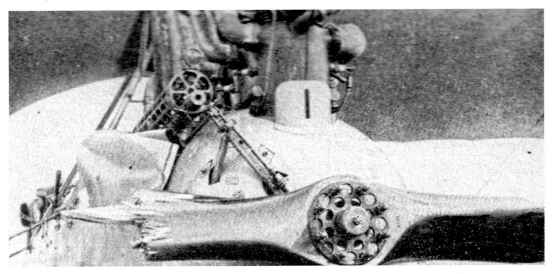

The propeller blade of an Albatros C.III was splintered from machine gun bullets when the synchronization gear malfunctioned.

Anthony Fokker (above), a Dutch airplane designer, developed a new aircraft for Germany's air force in 1915. The Fokker E.III, or "Eindecker" (one-wing), was a great advancement in military aviation. It was a nimble plane, as well as the first aircraft to be fitted with forward-firing machine guns synchronized to shoot between rotating propeller blades.

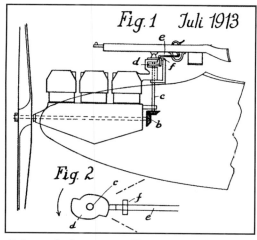

Schneider's patent illustration for his interrupter mechanism.

A year before the war started, German inventor Franz Schneider created a device that caused a machine gun to fire only after a propeller blade had passed safely by. It was called an interrupter mechanism. The German military showed little interest in Schneider's invention, and failed to use it in their aircraft.

French aircraft designer Raymond Saulnier also invented an interrupter mechanism, but it didn't work properly. In frustration, Saulnier wrapped sheets of metal around the edge of the propeller's blades. The metal deflected stray bullets that struck the propeller. The system worked, but it was crude, and hard on the engine. Also, bullets could ricochet and strike the plane or pilot.

In 1914, French pilot Roland Garros was using the deflector system on his plane when he crashed behind enemy lines. The German military took the deflector propeller and gave it to their brilliant Dutch-born aircraft designer Anthony Fokker.

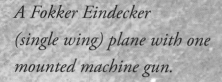

A Fokker Eindecker (single wing) plane with one mounted machine gun.

Fokker was unsatisfied with the deflector system. He worked to improve it. His synchronizing mechanism fired the machine gun only when the propeller blade wasn't in the line of fire. In May 1915, he put the new device on his latest aircraft design, the Fokker Eindecker monoplane (single wing). The aircraft was fitted with one or two synchronized Spandau machine guns. The Eindecker became a fearsome weapon in the hands of skilled pilots. It was slow, but it could outturn most other planes. It easily outclassed enemy aircraft like the British Bristol Scout D or the French Morane-Saulnier Type N. Hundreds of Allied planes were shot down by the superior Fokker Eindecker aircraft. This period of time became known as the "Fokker Scourge." It lasted through the end of 1915 and into the following year. Until then, the Germans ruled the skies.

DOGFIGHTS

By the end of 1915, British and French aircraft designers built planes that matched the dreaded German Eindecker. The French Nieuport and British De Havilland 2 were faster and more maneuverable than earlier planes. And by mid-1916, Allied planes were fitted with machine-gun synchronizers of their own.

Throughout the remaining years of the war, each side raced to invent sturdier planes that could fly higher and faster, and had better weapons. As the war years dragged on, dozens of new kinds of aircraft took to the sky. Many of them became legendary. The Germans rolled out the Albatros D.V and the Fokker Dr.I triplane. The Fokker D.VII biplane was considered by many pilots to be the best overall fighter of the war. The British developed the Sopwith Pup and the Sopwith Camel, while the French produced the Nieuport 17, the Spad VII, and Spad XIII. Many other planes—some good, some truly terrible in design—entered service during the war.

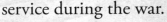

Fighter planes dueled over the battlefields. They made acrobatic turns and shot at each other in what became known as dogfights. Sometimes whole squadrons of planes would fight. Dozens of planes dodged in and out of a tight airspace while shooting at each other. A German unit led by Manfred von Richthofen, the Red Baron, was so skilled at flying in combat that it became known as the Flying Circus.

Flying during World War I was so new that combat techniques had to be learned in battle. German ace Oswald Boelcke led the first squadron, or *Jagdstaffel*, whose main job was to find and shoot down enemy planes. (*Jagdstaffel* is German for "hunting group.") Boelcke was a highly skilled pilot. He soon developed basic rules of air combat. They included keeping the sun at one's back in order to blind the enemy, always carrying through with an attack once it had begun, and firing only at close range when the target was within sight. The Allies came up with tactics of their own, including hiding in clouds and only attacking in superior numbers.

A favorite tactic was to dive on the enemy from above and shoot only when the target was very close. This kind of attack took steely nerves. If a pilot opened fire too soon, not only would he probably miss, he would also alert the enemy to his presence and ruin the element of surprise. The early rules of combat weren't too complicated. As Oswald Boelcke once said, "Well, it is quite simple. I fly close to my man, aim well, and then he falls down."

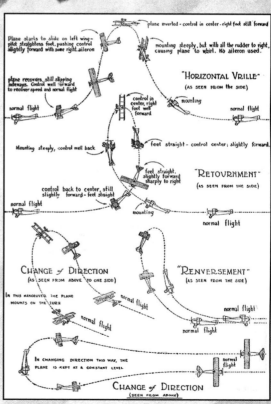

A page from American ace Eddie Rickenbacker's World War I memoirs.

HEAVY BOMBERS

A bomb is lobbed over the side of a WWI plane.

Planes were used to bomb ground targets during World War I, but not nearly as much as in following wars, especially World War II. During the first part of World War I, simple two-seater airplanes carried artillery shells. The person in the passenger seat would lob these over the side, hoping to hit something on the ground as they flew past. Needless to say, this was not very effective. Later, special bombs were made. Some were filled with high explosives. Others were incendiary bombs, used to burn down enemy buildings.

A German Gotha heavy bomber biplane strikes its target.

By the last part of the war, both sides were using large planes specially built to carry and drop bombs on the enemy. The British Handley Page 0/400 could carry a 2,000-pound (907-kg) payload of high explosives. It had a wingspan of about 100 feet (30 m), twice the length of an average city bus. The Russian Ilya Mourometz V was the first plane to use four engines.

The largest heavy bomber of the war was the German Zeppelin Staaken R.VI. This truly massive aircraft had a wingspan of 138 feet (42 m). With a crew of seven, it was armed with four to seven machine guns, and could carry up to 4,400 pounds (1,996 kg) of bombs. It could fly more than 14,000 feet (4,267 m) high, and stay in the air for almost 10 hours. It was often used to raid targets in London at night.

ZEPPELINS

Lighter-than-air technology was developed years before World War I began. Unlike airplanes, airships were sturdy, and could lift several tons of equipment. They also carried bombs to attack enemy targets on the ground.

Germany was the leader in airship design. Count Ferdinand von Zeppelin perfected a powered airship design in 1900. Zeppelins, as most airships came to be known, were huge, slow-moving machines with rigid, internal frames. The Zeppelin Company built gigantic machines that inspired awe as they passed overhead.

During the war, some Zeppelins measured more than 400 feet (122 m) long. Their great lifting power came from very buoyant—and extremely flammable—hydrogen gas.

Great Britain was first attacked by German airships in the spring of 1915. Germany was determined to disrupt English war factories, hoping this would shorten the war. At the beginning of World War I, Zeppelins could fly higher than airplanes. The first Zeppelins to bomb Britain crossed the English Channel on calm, moonlit nights with little fear of being shot down.

A crater in a Paris street from a 1916 Zeppelin bombing.

Zeppelins attack a ship-filled harbor in London.

The German bombing campaign didn't really affect the outcome of the war, but it brought terror to British citizens. Many people had never even seen an airplane before. The sight of a giant Zeppelin drifting across the night sky and dropping bombs on cities caused great panic. This was especially true in London and Paris, two prime targets of German bombing. There were more than 50 Zeppelin raids on Great Britain alone. Approximately 557 people were killed, and another 1,358 wounded.

As the war progressed, the Allies developed airplanes that had engines powerful enough to fly as high as Zeppelins. Unfortunately, the giant airships were not as easy to shoot down as one might expect. Many times bullets passed through without doing great harm. Also, Zeppelins were armed with machine guns to protect themselves.

New kinds of bullets were developed to help defeat the Zeppelin threat. Allied aircraft shot special incendiary ammunition at the slow-moving airships. The bullets were coated with phosphorus that was set aflame as they were shot from machine guns. After penetrating the Zeppelins' outer skin and inner compartments, they ignited the explosive hydrogen gas. This caused huge fireballs, which the Allied pilots had to swerve away from, or else they would meet the same deadly fate as the crew of the Zeppelins.

As more and more Zeppelins were shot down, Germany gradually stopped using them to bomb Britain. By the end of 1917, it was too dangerous to fly airships over enemy territory. Instead, airships and balloons were used through the remainder of the war as observation platforms for directing artillery, and especially for spotting submarines

ACES

Highly skilled aviators sometimes shot down dozens of enemy planes. These were the aces of World War I, brave and daring men whose very names made enemy pilots tremble.

The term "ace" first appeared in French newspapers in 1915. It was used to describe Adolphe Pegoud after he became the first pilot to shoot down five German aircraft. French aerial units began publishing the scores of pilots—the number of enemy aircraft they had shot down.

German pilot Oswald Boelcke was one of the world's first "aces." He is called the father of Germany's air force. He believed in formation fighting, rather than individual attacks. During World War I, he developed and taught rules of air combat to many new pilots.

Air combat was a deadly game. German ace Oswald Boelcke was killed after an in-air collision with one of his own men. Although he landed his damaged plane, he had failed to properly secure his safety belt. That, along with the fact that he didn't wear a helmet, resulted in his death on October 28, 1916, age 25.

Germany also started keeping track of its pilots' air victories, but they had to shoot down eight airplanes (later 16) before they became aces. The British and Americans followed the French example, giving their pilots the title of ace after five confirmed victories.

Only five percent of World War I pilots achieved the status of ace. They became celebrities in their home countries. Regular soldiers, stranded in the mud of the Western Front, greatly admired the aces. They were eager to read about the daring pilots' adventures high above in the wild blue yonder.

René Fonck

"I put my bullets into the target as if I placed them there by hand."

RENÉ FONCK

René Fonck of France was the highest scoring French ace of World War I. He scored 75 kills. He claimed to have shot down 127 enemy aircraft, but only 75 were verified and entered into the record books.

Fonck was a gifted pilot whose favorite tactic was to fly very close to the enemy before firing. He shot down many airplanes on the first try using this method. Fonck said, "I put my bullets into the target as if I placed them there by hand." On two separate occasions, Fonck shot down six German planes in one day.

René Fonck was the top-scoring Allied fighter ace of World War I. Fonck did not like dogfighting, but preferred to hold back, stalking his target, and only striking when the time was right. An excellent marksman, he used his machine guns to bring down 75 enemy planes over the course of the war.

Unlike most aces, Fonck survived the war. He would have been a popular national hero, but his personality was very irritating, and he could be a show-off. A friend once said of Fonck, "He is a tiresome braggart and even a bore, but in the air, a slashing rapier, a steel blade tempered with unblemished courage and priceless skill…"

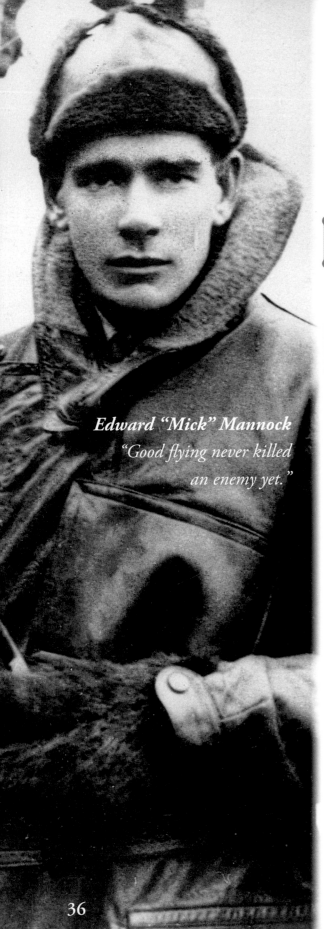

Edward "Mick" Mannock
"Good flying never killed an enemy yet."

EDWARD "MICK" MANNOCK

Edward "Mick" Mannock of Great Britain scored 61 victories in World War I. He joined the British air services in 1916. It was a time when war in the air was going through big changes. No longer a dashing, chivalrous pastime, air war became more ruthless as pilots concentrated on shooting down the enemy.

In 1914, Turkey joined the Central Powers, aligning itself with Germany and Austria-Hungary. Mannock had been in the country working for a British phone company. He was thrown into prison, where he was abused. On the verge of death, he was finally sent home to Britain.

Mick Mannock joined the Royal Flying Corps (RFC) in 1916. After training, he scored his first combat victory on May 7, 1917.

Perhaps because of his mistreatment in prison, Mannock despised Germans, especially when he read of atrocities committed against Belgian civilians by German soldiers. After joining the air service, Mannock's rage drove him to shoot down as many German planes as possible. By the end of 1917, he had already scored 23 victories. Mannock showed no mercy in the air. He once said, "The swines are better dead—no prisoners!"

Mannock had great skill as a pilot. He was also much admired by the men who served with him. Many considered him the best flight leader of the war. German aircraft never once surprised his flights.

Mannock died in July 1918. He was flying low after following one of his victims to watch him crash. A soldier on the ground shot at Mannock's plane and struck the fuel tank. The plane burst into flames and nosedived into no-man's-land. His body was found by the Germans, but was never recovered by the Allies. It is unknown where he was buried.

A year after his death, Mannock was posthumously awarded the Victoria Cross, Britain's highest military award for bravery. During the ceremony, Mannock was called "an outstanding example of fearless courage, remarkable skill, devotion to duty and self-sacrifice, which has never been surpassed."

Victoria Cross

Eddie Rickenbacker

"Courage is doing what you are afraid to do. There can be no courage unless you are scared."

EDWARD "EDDIE" RICKENBACKER

 Edward "Eddie" Rickenbacker of the United States was a professional race car driver when the war began. He had driven in the first Indianapolis 500, and also set a speed record of 134 miles per hour (216 kph) in Daytona Beach, Florida. In 1917, Eddie Rickenbacker was a sergeant in France, driving General John Pershing's staff car.

One frequent passenger was General William "Billy" Mitchell, commander of the U.S. flying corps. It was Mitchell who convinced General Pershing that Rickenbacker would be more valuable as a pilot than a chauffeur. After attending flight school, Rickenbacker became a skilled pilot and brilliant tactical fighter.

Rickenbacker's talents soon placed him in charge of the 94th Aero Pursuit Squadron. It was also called the "Hat in the Ring Squadron" because of its distinctive insignia.

Rickenbacker was a brave pilot, but he wasn't reckless. He liked to patiently position himself above the enemy, with the sun at his back, then quickly dive down, guns blazing at the last moment. By the end of the war, Rickenbacker scored 26 victories, many against Manfred von Richthofen's Flying Circus. For his exploits in the air, Rickenbacker earned a Congressional Medal of Honor.

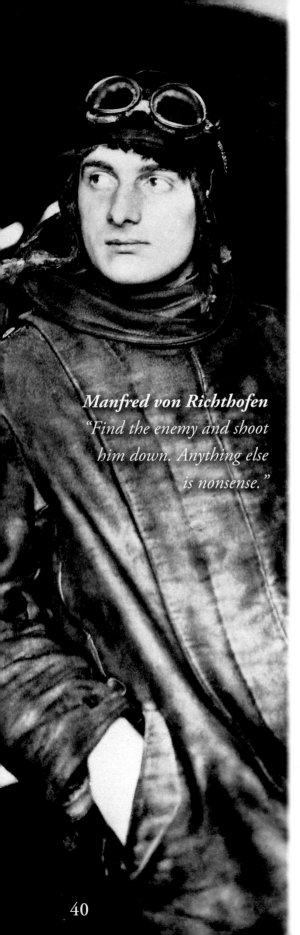

Manfred von Richthofen
"Find the enemy and shoot him down. Anything else is nonsense."

MANFRED VON RICHTHOFEN

By far the most famous and successful ace of World War I was Germany's Manfred von Richthofen. He scored 80 confirmed air victories, more than any other pilot in the war.

Richthofen was born to a noble German family. His father wanted him to become an army officer, but young Manfred was more interested in horses and gymnastics. Shortly after the war began, Richthofen was stationed in the trenches. He managed to get a transfer to the air service, and by the end of 1915 had earned his pilot license.

Richthofen wasn't a naturally gifted flyer. He even crashed during his first flight at the controls. However, he quickly learned the skills necessary for fighting in the air. Under the direction of German ace Oswald Boelcke, Richthofen quickly scored many victories.

Richthofen was given command of his own squadron, Jasta 2, in January 1917. Shortly after that he commanded Jasta 11.

Richthofen's fame spread as he scored victory after victory. Many pilots in his squadron were inexperienced. In order to more easily identify him during combat, Richthofen

The Jasta 11 squadron of Albatros D.III fighters. Richthofen's famous red plane is second in line from the front.

had his Albatros biplane painted bright red. Some said he also had the plane painted red to taunt or frighten his opponents. Allied pilots began calling Richthofen the Red Baron.

Richthofen wrote about the following air battle in his logbook on April 2, 1917: "Together with Lieutenants Voss and Lothar von Richthofen, I attacked an enemy squadron of eight Sopwiths above a closed cover of clouds on the enemy's side of the lines. The plane I had singled out was driven away from its formation and tried to escape me by hiding in the clouds after I had put holes in its gasoline tanks.

"Below the clouds, I immediately attacked him again, thereby forcing him to land 300 yards east of Givenchy. But as yet my adversary would not surrender, and even as his machine was on the ground, he kept shooting at me, thereby hitting my machine very severely when I was only five yards off the ground.

"Consequently, I attacked him already on the ground and killed one of the occupants."

In June 1917, Richthofen commanded a group of about 50 of Germany's best pilots. Officially, the group was called JG1, but it soon became known as the Flying Circus. They took off in huge V formations, with Richthofen in the lead in his red plane, striking fear into Allied pilots.

On July 6, 1917, Richthofen crashed. He survived, but suffered a severe head wound. When he returned to service, his plane had been replaced with a Fokker Dr.I triplane. The Dr.I was very maneuverable. In the hands of a skilled pilot like Richthofen, it was a deadly flying machine. By April 1918, Richthofen scored his 80th air victory, more than any other pilot.

Richthofen was killed in a dogfight on April 21, 1918, by Canadian pilot Captain Arthur "Roy" Brown. The Red Baron had been chasing an Allied plane and didn't notice Brown's Sopwith Camel trailing behind in the confusion of the dogfight. Brown fired a single burst at the red triplane, then veered off as Richthofen's plane made a rough landing.

Australian troops quickly arrived at the scene and were amazed to find Richthofen in the wreckage, gravely wounded by a single bullet to the chest. He soon died. There is some controversy as to whether Richthofen was struck by Australian ground troops, but credit is usually given to Brown for the victory over the Red Baron.

Richthofen was buried with full military honors the next day in Bertangles, France, by British and Australian troops. Germany mourned the loss of its famous ace. After the war, in 1925, Richthofen's body was reburied in Berlin, Germany. In 1975, it was moved once more, this time to the Richthofen family plot in a cemetery in Wiesbaden, Germany.

■ Central Powers	Famous Aces of WWI	■ Allied Nations
Pilot	**Country**	**Victories**
Manfred von Richthofen	Germany	80
René Fonck	France	75
William "Billy" Bishop	Canada	72
Raymond Collishaw	Canada	62
Ernst Udet	Germany	62
Edward "Mick" Mannock	United Kingdom	61
James McCudden	United Kingdom	57
Andrew Beauchamp-Proctor	South Africa	54
Erich Loewenhardt	Germany	53
Albert Ball	United Kingdom	44
Edward "Eddie" Rickenbacker	United States	26
Max Immelmann	Germany	15

TIMELINE

June 28: Austria-Hungary's Archduke Franz Ferdinand is assassinated by a Serbian nationalist while touring Sarajevo, the capital of Bosnia-Herzegovina.

August: World War I fighting begins as German armed forces invade Belgium and France.

August 26-31: Russia suffers a major defeat at Battle of Tannenberg.

September 9-14: Second massive Russian defeat, this time at Battle of the Masurian Lakes.

Spring: German Zeppelins launch bombing raids against English cities.

April 22: Germans are first to use lethal poison gas on a large scale during the Battle of Ypres.

May: Anthony Fokker designs synchronized machine guns for his E.III Eindecker airplane.

May 7: A German U-boat sinks the unarmed British passenger liner *Lusitania*, killing 1,198 people, including 128 Americans. The American public is outraged, but President Wilson manages to keep the U.S. neutral.

Feb 21-Dec 18: Battle of Verdun. Nearly one million soldiers are killed or wounded.

June 24-Nov 13: Battle of the Somme costs approximately 1.25 million casualties. On July 1, the first day of the infantry attack, British forces suffered a staggering 60,000 casualties, including 20,000 dead, the largest single-day casualty total in British military history. Many troops are killed by a new battlefield weapon, the machine gun.

January 31:	Germany declares unrestricted submarine warfare, outraging the American public.
March 12:	The Russian Revolution overthrows Czar Nicholas II. The country is taken over by Lenin's communist government during the Bolshevik Revolution on November 7.
April 6:	The United States declares war on Germany.
June:	Manfred von Richthofen takes command of JG1, which would become known as the Flying Circus.
December 15:	Russia's Bolshevik government agrees to a separate peace with Germany, taking Russia out of the war.

March 21-July 19:	Germany mounts five "Ludendorff offensives" against strengthening Allied forces. The attacks are costly to both sides, but Germany fails to crush the Allied armies.
April 21:	Manfred von Richthofen is shot down and killed after a military career in which he scored 80 confirmed victories, more than any other pilot of World War I.
May 30-June 17:	American forces are successful against the Germans at Chateau-Thierry and Belleau Woods.
July:	British ace Edward Mannock is shot down and killed.
Sept 26-Nov 11:	French and American forces launch the successful Meuse-Argonne Offensive.
Sept 27-Oct 17:	British forces break through the Hindenburg Line.
November 11:	Armistice Day. Fighting stops at 11:00 AM.

May 7-June 28:	The Treaty of Versailles is written and signed.

GLOSSARY

ALLIES

Great Britain, France, and Russia formed the Allies in 1914 at the outbreak of World War I. Japan also joined the Allies, but played a minor role. Russia dropped out of the war in 1917. Italy joined the Allies in 1916, followed by the United States in 1917.

BIPLANE

A plane that has two sets of wings, one on top of the other.

CENTRAL POWERS

In World War I, the countries fighting against the Allies: Germany, Austria-Hungary, Turkey, and Bulgaria.

CONGRESSIONAL MEDAL OF HONOR

The U.S. military's highest decoration, awarded by Congress for "gallantry at the risk of life above and beyond the call of duty."

DOGFIGHT

Air-to-air combat between opposing sides of aircraft.

FUSELAGE

The main body of an airplane, not including the wings, tail, or engine.

INCENDIARY BULLETS AND BOMBS

Bullets and bombs designed to start fires on impact. They are often loaded with flammable material, like phosphorous. Airplanes often used incendiary bullets against Zeppelins in order to set them on fire and force them down.

MONOPLANE

A plane with a single set of wings. The Fokker E.III Eindecker is a monoplane.

No-Man's-Land

The area of land between two opposing lines of trenches.

Posthumous

Arising or continuing after one's death. In the military, to be awarded a medal posthumously means to be honored after death.

Reconnaissance

To explore or scout the enemy's position. Aircraft in World War I were very useful in discovering the enemy's exact location, which helped make artillery fire more accurate. As both sides began to realize the importance of aerial reconnaissance, they each developed fighter aircraft to shoot down enemy reconnaissance planes.

Triplane

A plane that has three sets of wings stacked on top of each other. At one point in his career, Manfred von Richthofen flew a blood-red Fokker Dr.I triplane.

Western Front

Established by December 1914, the Western Front was a network of trenches that stretched across eastern France and a section of western Belgium. The Western Front ran approximately 400 miles (644 km), reaching from the North Sea to the border of Switzerland.

To learn more about the aircraft of World War I, visit abdobooklinks.com. These links are routinely monitored and updated to provide the most current information available.

INDEX